Handwriting

Collins Photocopy

PRINT SCRIPT

Peter Smith & Judith Williams

© Collins Educational 1988

First published in 1988 by Holmes McDougall Ltd., Edinburgh

This edition published 1990 by Collins Educational, London and Glasgow

ISBN 0 00 314254 X

Printed by Antony Rowe, Chippenham.

CONTENTS

Teachers' Notes

PRINT SCRIPT

Numerous inter-related skills go to make up the process of learning to write. Good eye/hand co-ordination and control are essential. Visual discrimination must be sharp and the visual memory keen. There are many activities designed to promote these skills. Some of them are described in the introduction to Handwriting *Pre-Writing Skills*. Moreover, *Pre-Writing Skills* provides pre-writing practice of all the essential movements of print script by means of drawings and patterns, and, by association with familiar objects, attempts to fix the basic writing patterns in the child's visual memory.

The child also needs to understand that the written word is the sounds of speech represented on paper by a set code of symbols. As Diack says, "A word is a time-chart of sound".

Sound/Symbol relationship
We must teach children the code, i.e. the sound/symbol relationship, otherwise they will never crack it and reading and writing will remain a mystery to them. The teacher has to help the child to focus attention on sounds within words, and has to develop in the child the ability to hear, isolate and reproduce required phonetic sounds in speech and their correct sequence in word form. Recognition of the sound/symbols and how to reproduce them, that is, to write the letters of the alphabet in various combinations, also has to be taught.

Letter formation
When children first copy the teacher's writing they make an approximation to the model. It may be similar to the original in appearance but, in fact, have been constructed very differently. However correct letter formation must be taught and good writing habits formed early. Bad writing habits will be a hindrance later on, especially when children come to cursive writing, and will have to be unlearned. It is frustrating and demoralising to have to back-track in this way.

Children enjoy handwriting practice. They derive satisfaction from mastery of this complex skill. The worksheets in this book present each letter of print script for the child to go over and reproduce, and instructions and indication for the correct way to form each letter.

Sequence of movement
The pages are arranged so that as far as possible the child reproduces letters under a good model each time rather than underneath the pupil's own possible mistakes. Every effort has been made to focus attention on the correct sequence of movement, and the relationship of one letter to another, and to help to cope with ascenders like "d" and descenders like "p" and "g".

Letters should be formed in one movement whenever possible. The pencils should move in a continuous flow, without pausing or lifting until the letter is complete. There are a few exceptions to this rule:- f, k, t, x, and y. Do not allow the child to go back and forth repeatedly over pencil strokes.

'R2', the robot, indicates where on each page to start, and the magic pencil shows where on each letter to begin. The arrows indicate in which direction to pencil should move.

Preparing to write
Before the children begin to write, check that they are sitting comfortably at their work-tables, that the paper is suitably positioned and the pencil grip is correct. A left-handed child needs a soft pencil, which will flow easily over the paper, and which should be held further away from its point so that the marks it makes can be easily seen, and to prevent the pencil being gripped too tightly. The sheet of paper should be placed more to the left, so that the child is not writing across his or her own body.

Discussion
The child will derive great benefit from first discussing with you the page to be worked, and establishing the sound value of the symbols upon it. It will also help if you watch the letters being traced with a finger to check that it is being done correctly before the child picks up the pencil.

Notes for specific pages
Worksheets 11 and 12

Please note that in this scheme "q" and "y" have straight tails to conform with the Link-Up Reading Scheme (published by Collins Educational).

Related teaching ideas
"Fun with Sounds"

Sometimes it helps children to remember the sound value of the symbol if it is associated with a familiar sound or experience from their lives, or from a film or T.V. A story can be woven around the association. A few suggestions:—

1.	a-a	— the raised finger of admonition
2.	b-b-b	— a motor-boat engine
3.	'c'	— a catch closing e.g. on a cupboard
4.	d-d-d-d	— a dripping tap
5.	e-e-e	— villainous laughter or sheep bleating
6.	f-f-f-f	— bicycle pump
7.	g-g-g-g-g	— bottle pouring
8.	h-h-h-h-h	— dog panting
9.	i-i-i-i-i	— mouse squeaking
10.	j-j-j-j-j	— steam-engine
11.	k-k-k-k	— I'm stuck. Can *you* think of anything
12.	l-l-l	— wolves howling
13.	m-m-m!	— Nice!
14.	n-n-n!	— Wrinkled nose! Don't like you!
15.	o-o	— motor-horn
16.	p-p-p	— puffing on a pipe
17.	q-q-q	— snooker balls hitting
18.	r-r-r	— rocket taking off
19.	s-s-s	— snake
20.	t-t-t	— testing air-pressure on car tyre. Putting air into a car tyre under pressure.
21.	-u-!	— punch in the stomach
22.	v-v-v	— model aeroplane
23.	w-w-w	— whip
24.	x-x-x-x	— whispering
25.	y-y-y	— why
26.	z-z-z	— fly buzzing

Assessment of Handwriting

Just as it is widely recognised that there is a need for a policy for handwriting in primary and middle schools so it must surely be accepted that it is necessary to include arrangements for assessment of the results of the policy. There are two aspects of assessment to be considered:

1. Subjective Broad Assessment

This may be based on perusal of children's work or on observation of the children when writing. Probably, a combination of both approaches is necessary as it is important to assess the actual process of writing as well as the finished product.

Although this kind of broad assessment is relatively informal and highly subjective it is still necessary to arrange to carry it out at regular intervals, perhaps once a term or once a year. One member of staff should be designated with the responsibility of ensuring that the assessment does happen. It is also helpful for staff to agree on a list of criteria by which handwriting is to be judged. The following suggestions might form the basis for such a list.

Criteria for Broad Assessment

1 That the children's writing is legible when written at different speeds as appropriate to different purposes.
2 That the children's writing is pleasant to look at and that it leads to the development of individual styles.
3 That all letters appear to be started in the correct place and to be formed correctly.
4 That, when writing, the children adopt sensible postures, hold writing instruments acceptably and position their papers sensibly.
5 That letters are of constant size with ascenders and descenders appropriately differentiated.
6 That vertical and diagonal strokes are parallel.
7 That spaces between letters and spaces between words are appropriate and constant.

2. Diagnostic assessment of Individuals

Pupil records often indicate unsatisfactory standards of achievement in the skill of handwriting but, all to frequently, they fail to provide diagnostic detail. It is to be hoped that, in schools, where handwriting is taught thoroughly, few children will give sufficient concern to require detailed diagnostic assessment. For those who do, a record sheet can be used to guide observation and to provide a basis for teaching. The sheet would require amendment as the pupil develops.

Diagnostic Schedule

There are three main aspects of handwriting requiring attention:

a) Posture and Pencil Grip etc.
Questions to be asked here include:

i) Is the child sitting comfortably at a table of appropriate size?
ii) Does the child hold the pencil in a helpful manner i.e. using thumb and next two fingers in an appropriate grip?
iii) Is the writing paper correctly positioned?

b) Letter Formation
It is convenient to consider letters in family groups as they relate to writing patterns. Questions to be answered through observation for each family include:

i) Can the child execute the related pattern satisfactorily?
ii) Does the child commence making the letters at the right place?
iii) Does the child make the letters correctly?
iv) Does the child close the letters when necessary?
v) Does the child differentiate ascenders and decenders adequately?
vi) Are there reversal/inversal problems?

FAMILIES

c) Presentation

Questions to be asked here include:

i) Is the size of writing appropriate?
ii) Can the child write acceptably on plain paper?
iii) Does the child use lines appropriately when using lined paper?
iv) Are vertical strokes parallel?
v) Are diagonal strokes parallel?
vi) Is the spacing between letters and spacing between words consistent and appropriate?
vii) Can the child make capital letters correctly?
viii) If not, which capital letters give difficulty?

It is possible to devise and duplicate a school checksheet based on these criteria. A published handwriting checklist along similar lines can be obtained from LDA, Duke Street, Wisbech, Cambridgeshire PE13 2AE.

Worksheet 1

Preparation for v, w

Name _____

Go over the zig-zag shape and finish it.

Then go over the v shapes and finish them.

Now go over the w shapes and finish them. Follow the arrows each time.

Worksheet 2

Preparation for n, m

Name _____

Go over the bridge shape and finish it.

Then go over the n shapes and finish them.

Now go over the m shapes and finish them. Follow the arrows each time.

Print Script

Worksheet 3

Preparation for h, r

Name _____

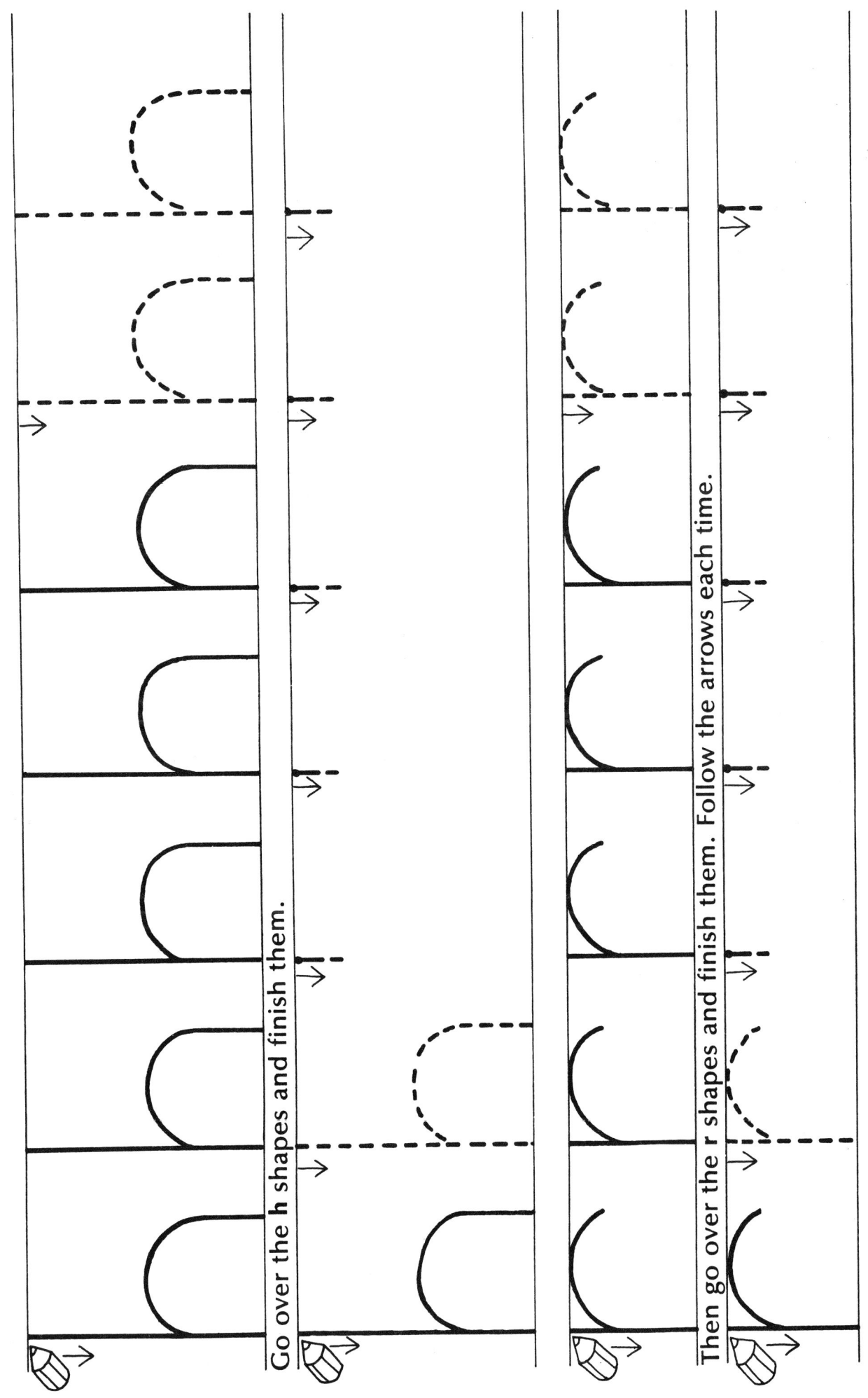

Go over the h shapes and finish them.

Then go over the r shapes and finish them. Follow the arrows each time.

Worksheet 4

Preparation for l, f

Worksheet 4

Name _____

Go over the l shapes and finish them.

Then go over the f shapes and finish them. These have two separate lines. Follow the arrows each time.

Print Script

You may photocopy this page for use within the classroom. © Collins Educational

Worksheet 5

Preparation for t, u

Name

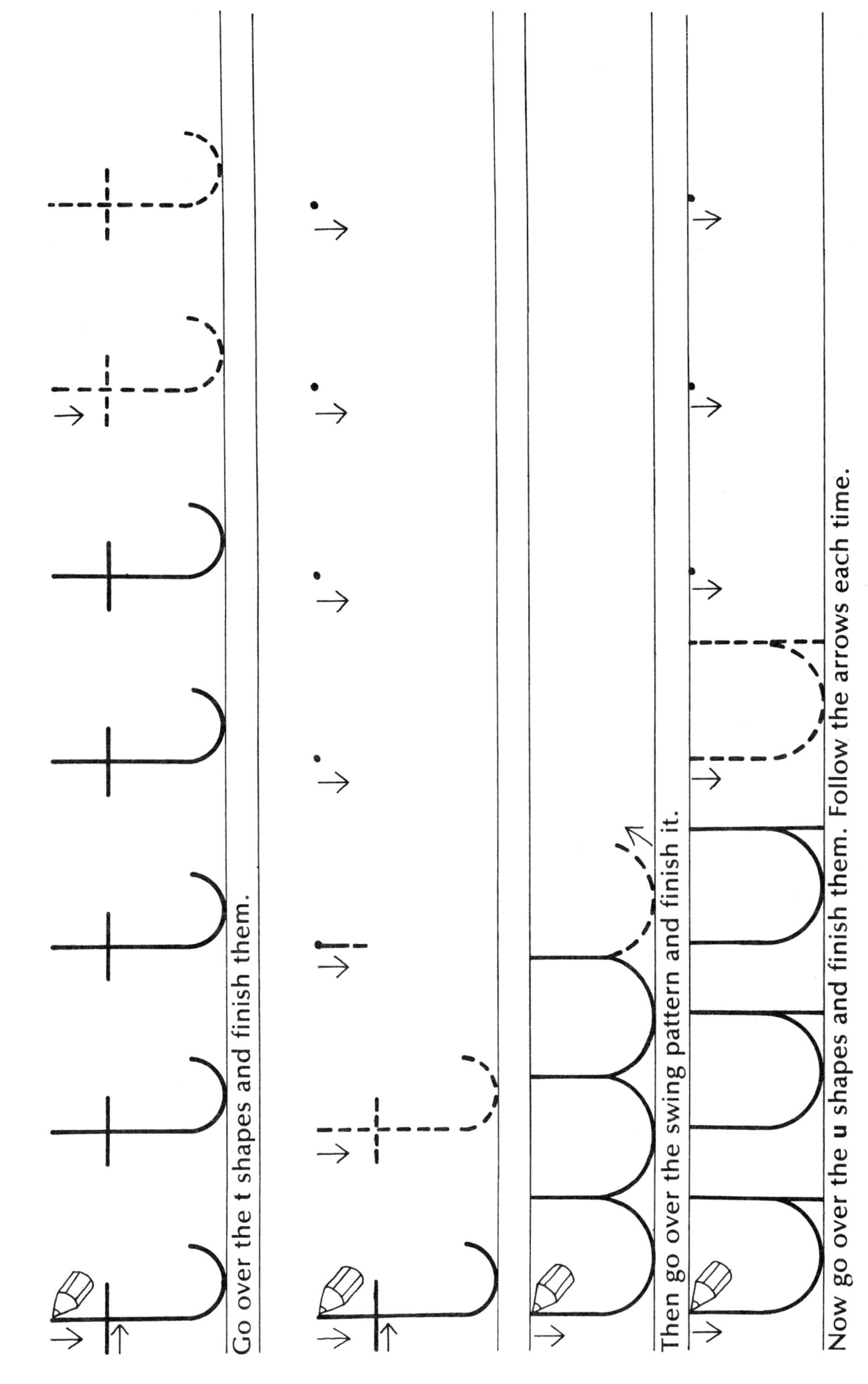

Go over the t shapes and finish them.

Then go over the swing pattern and finish it.

Now go over the u shapes and finish them. Follow the arrows each time.

Worksheet 6

Preparation for c, e

Name _____

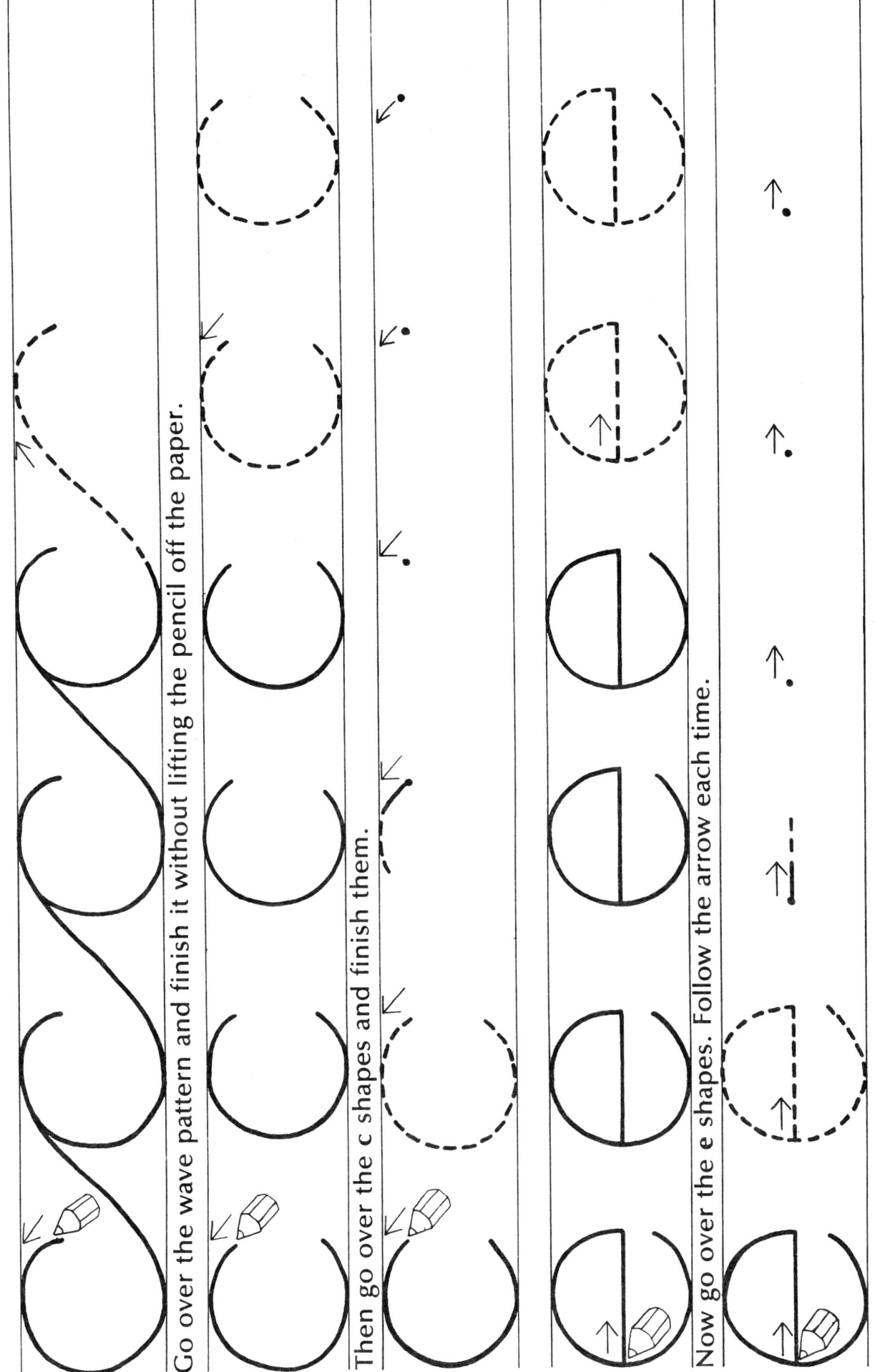

Go over the wave pattern and finish it without lifting the pencil off the paper.

Then go over the c shapes and finish them.

Now go over the e shapes. Follow the arrow each time.

Worksheet 7

Preparation for c, o, e

Name _____

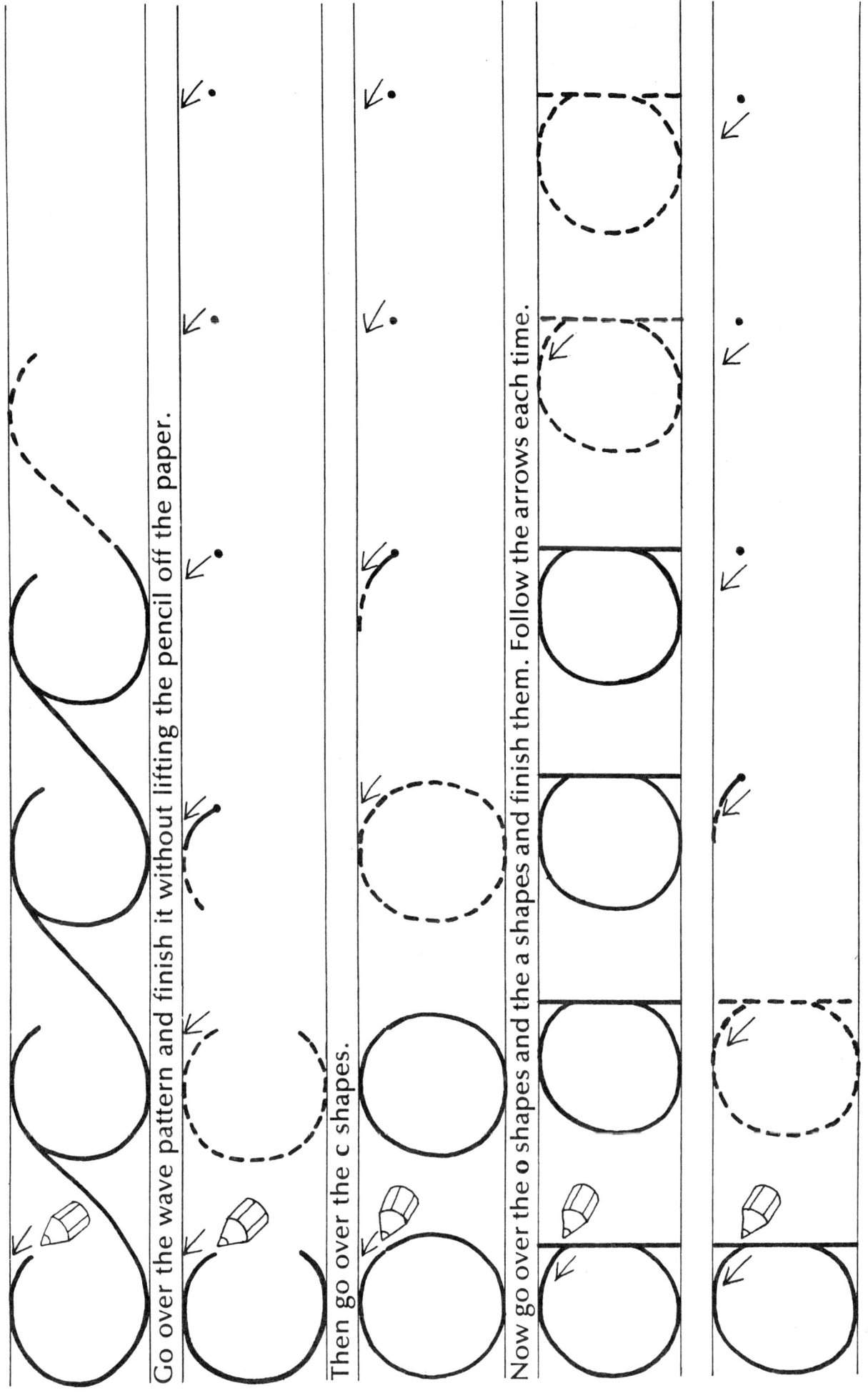

Go over the wave pattern and finish it without lifting the pencil off the paper.

Then go over the c shapes.

Now go over the o shapes and the a shapes and finish them. Follow the arrows each time.

Print Script

Worksheet 8

Preparation for d, a

Name

Go over the **d** shapes and finish them. Remember to follow the arrows.

Then go over the **a** shapes and finish them. Each letter should be done without lifting the pencil off the paper.

Worksheet 9

Preparation for k, x

Name _____

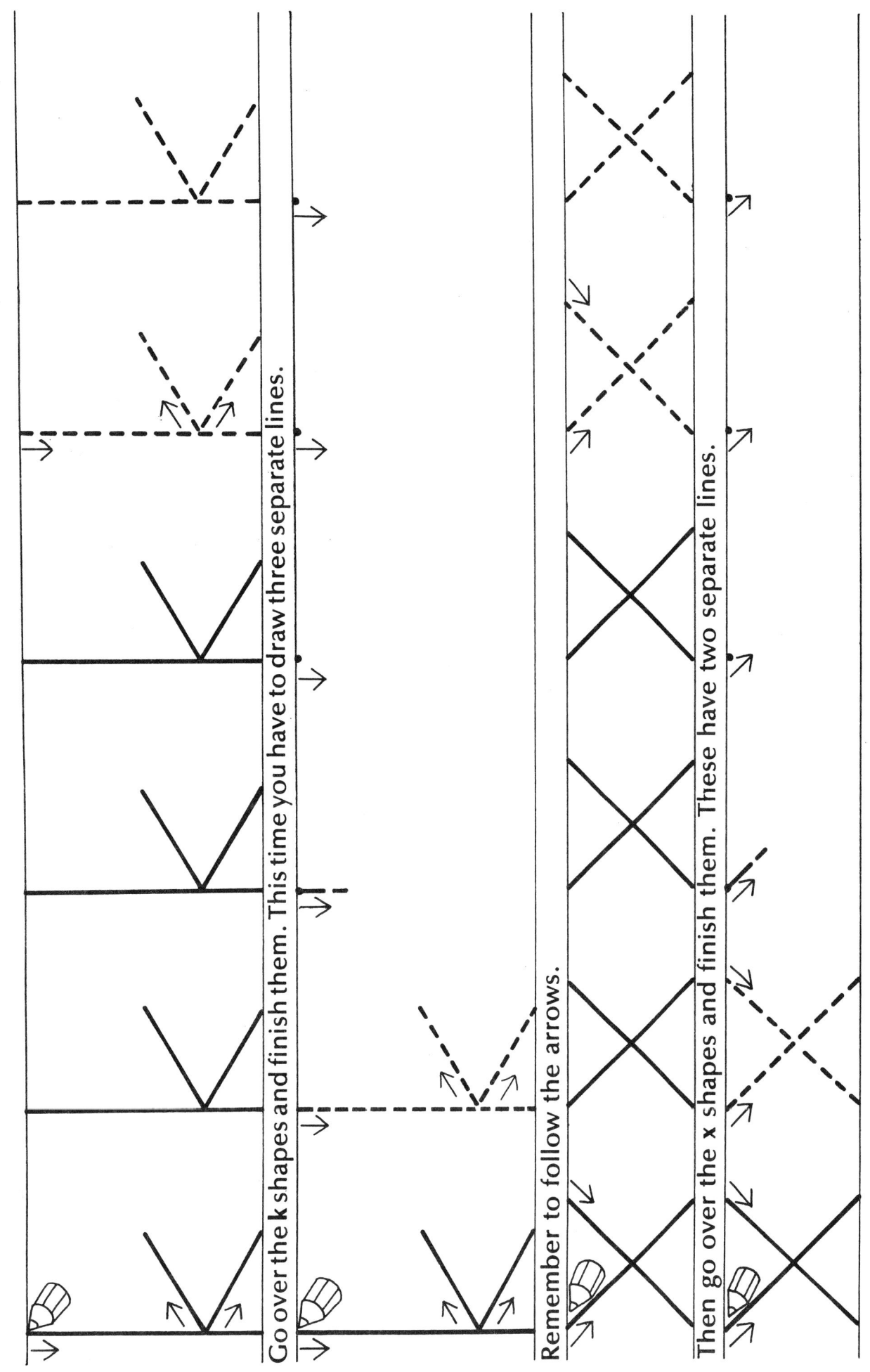

Go over the **k** shapes and finish them. This time you have to draw three separate lines.

Remember to follow the arrows.

Then go over the **x** shapes and finish them. These have two separate lines.

Print Script

Worksheet 10

Preparation for s, z

Name _____

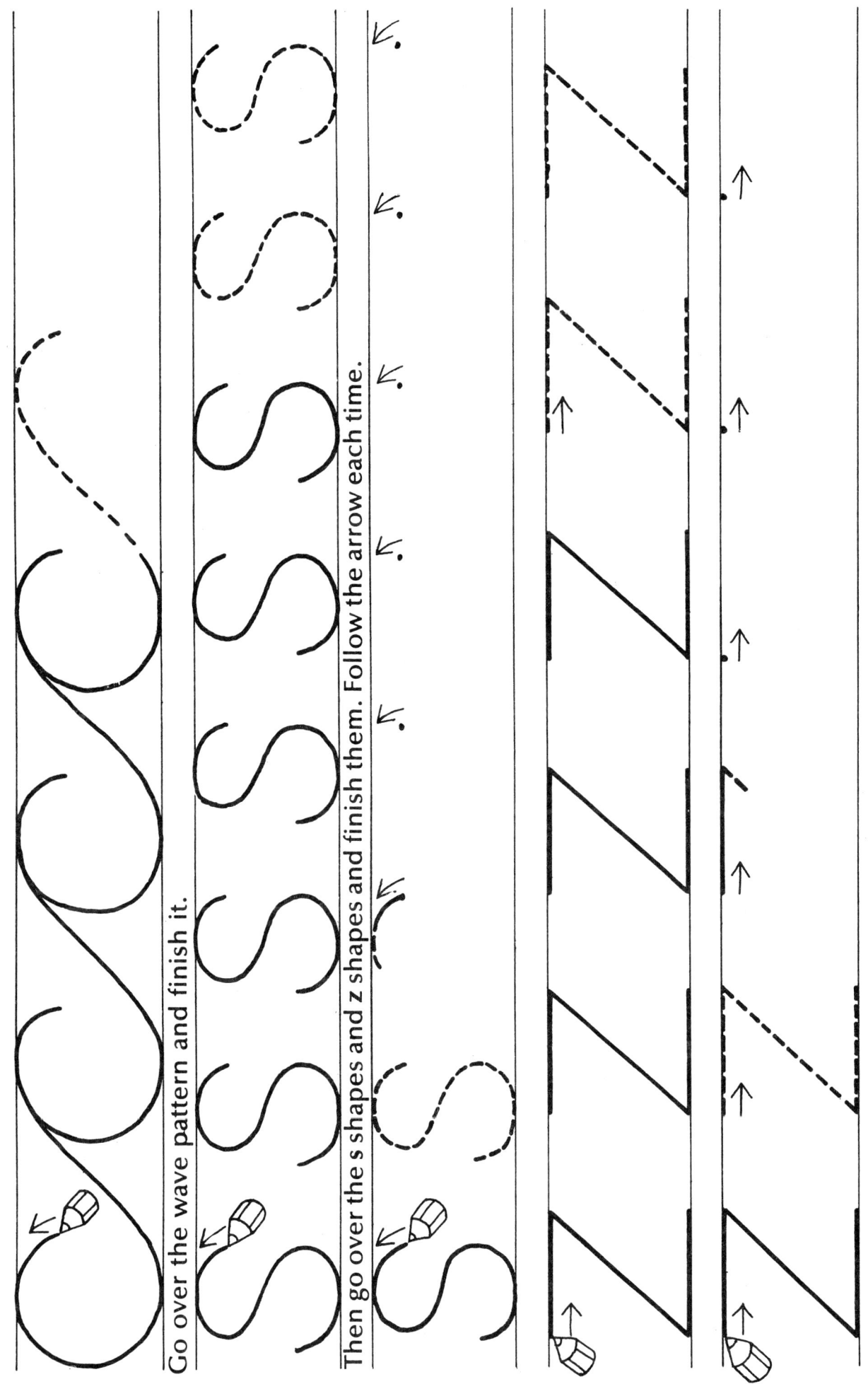

Go over the wave pattern and finish it.

Then go over the s shapes and z shapes and finish them. Follow the arrow each time.

Worksheet 11

Preparation for q, g

Name _____

Go over each **q** shape and finish it without lifting the pencil off the paper.

Then go over the **g** shapes and finish them. Remember to follow the arrows each time.

Worksheet 12

Preparation for i, j, y

Name _____

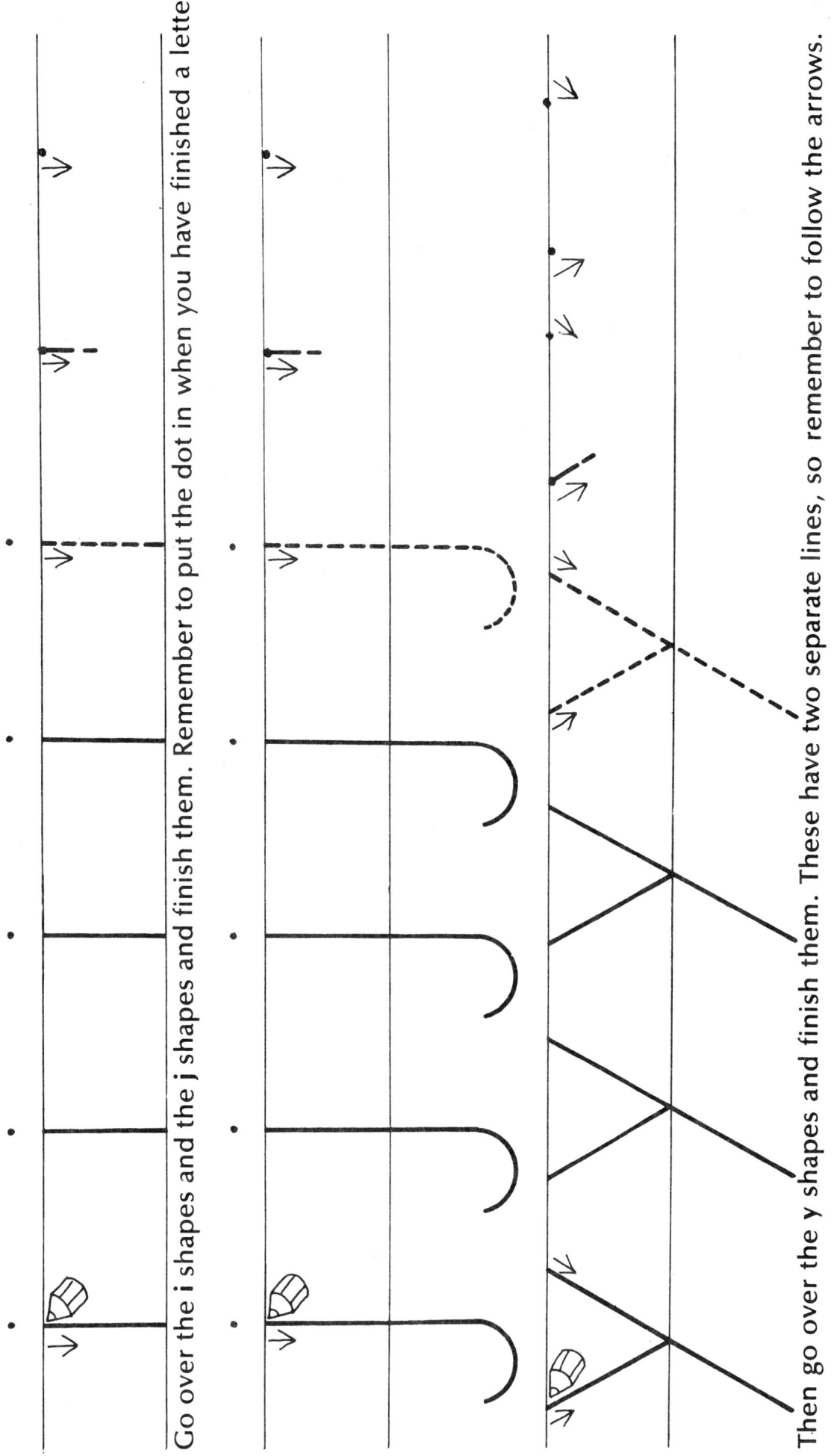

Go over the i shapes and the j shapes and finish them. Remember to put the dot in when you have finished a letter.

Then go over the y shapes and finish them. These have two separate lines, so remember to follow the arrows.

Worksheet 13

Preparation for b, p

Name

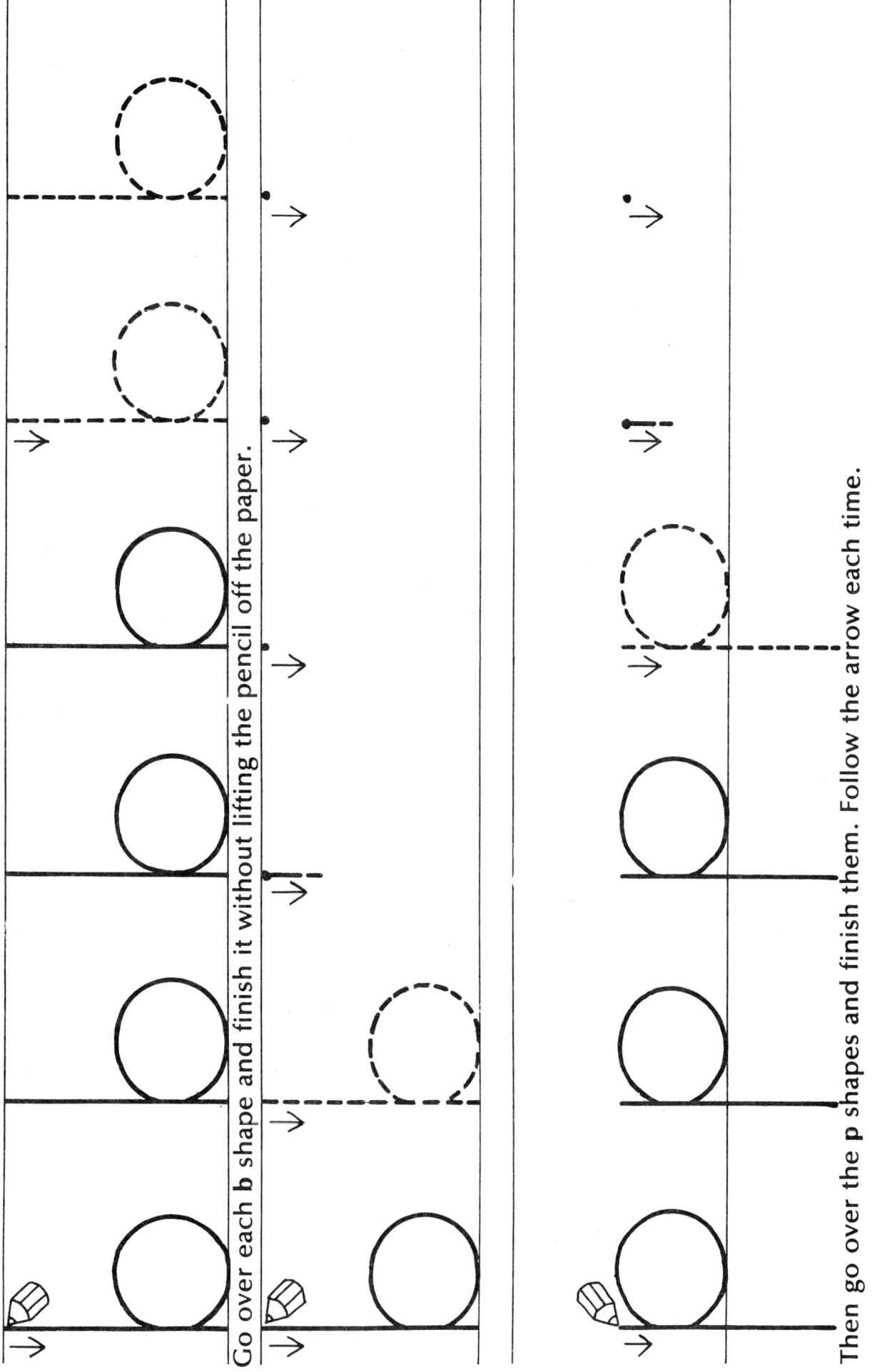

Go over each **b** shape and finish it without lifting the pencil off the paper.

Then go over the **p** shapes and finish them. Follow the arrow each time.

Print Script

Worksheet 14

Bridge pattern reversed — r, n, m, h
Tooth pattern revised — v, w, y

 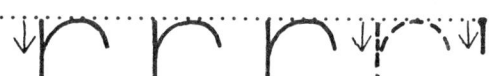

Go over the bridges pattern, then go over the **r** shapes and finish them.

Go over the **n** shapes and finish them.

Now go over the **m** shapes and the **h** shapes and finish them.

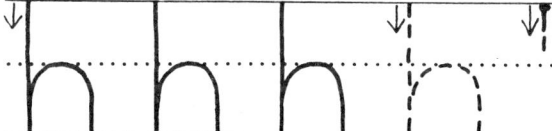

Go over the tooth pattern and finish it.

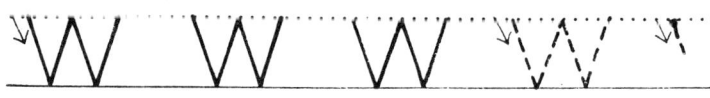

Now go over the **v w** and **y** shapes and finish them.

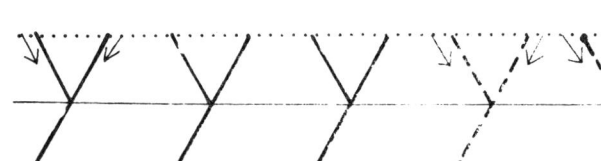

Worksheet 15

Letters based on horizontal, vertical and diagonal
strokes
Extra practice for s

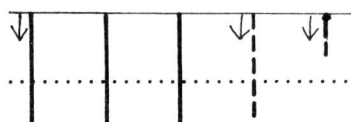

Go over the **l** shapes and finish them.

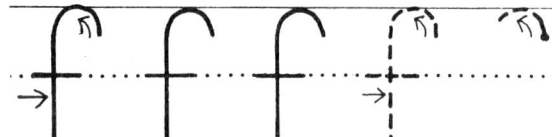

Now go over the **f**, **k** and **x** shapes and finish them.

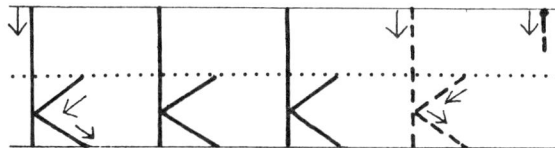

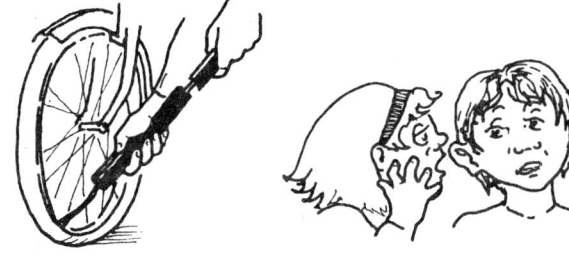  

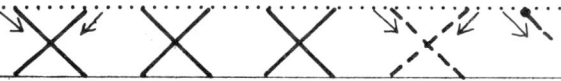

Go over the **z** shapes and finish them.

Now go over the **i**, **j** and **s** shapes and finish them.

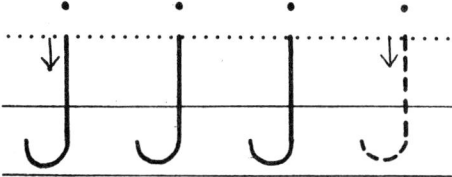

Worksheet 16

Swings pattern revised — u, t
Wave pattern revised — b, p
Extra practice for S and P

Go over the swings pattern and finish it.

Now go over the **u**, **t** and **s** shapes and finish them.

Go over the weave pattern and finish it.

Now go over the **b**, **p** and **s** shapes and finish them.

You may photocopy this page for use within the classroom. © Collins Educational

Worksheet 17

Wave pattern revised — g, e, o, a, d, g, q

Go over the wave pattern and finish it.

Now go over the **c**, **e** and **o** shapes and finish them.

Go over the **a** shapes and finish them.

Now go over the **d**, **g** and **q** shapes and finish them.

You may photocopy this page for use within the classroom. © Collins Educational

Worksheet 18

Capital letters beside lower case versions — v, w, y, n, m, h, r

Name ______________________________ Worksheet 18

Vv Vv

Go over the big **V** and little **v** shapes and finish them.

Ww Ww

Now go over the big **W**, little **w**, big **Y** and little **y** shapes.

Yy Yy Yy Yy Yy

Yy Yy

Nn Nn

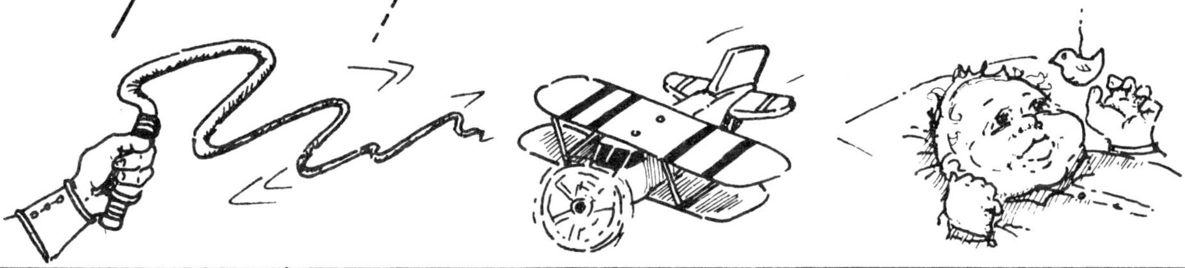

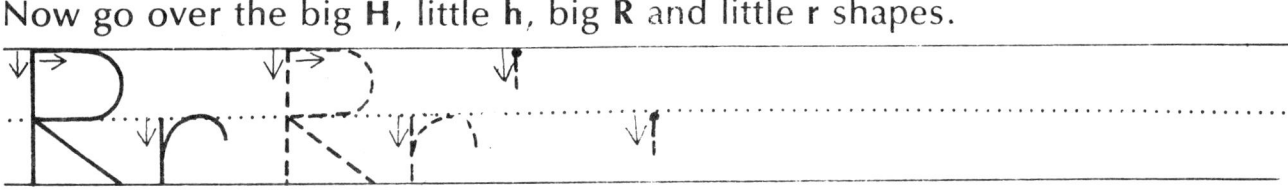

Go over the big **N** and little **n** shapes and finish them.

Mm Mm

Go over the big **M** and little **m** shapes and finish them.

Hh Hh

Now go over the big **H**, little **h**, big **R** and little **r** shapes.

Rr Rr

Worksheet 19

Capital letters beside lower case versions — l, f, k, x, z, i, j, s

Go over the big **L** and little **l** shapes and finish them.

Go over the **big F** and little **f** shapes and finish them.

Now go **over and** finish the big **K**, little **k**, big **X** and little **x** shapes.

Go over the **big Z** and little **z** shapes.

Now go over and finish the big **I**, little **i**, big **J**, little **j**, big **S** and little **s** shapes.

Worksheet 20

Capital letters beside lower case versions — c, e, t, u, s, b, p

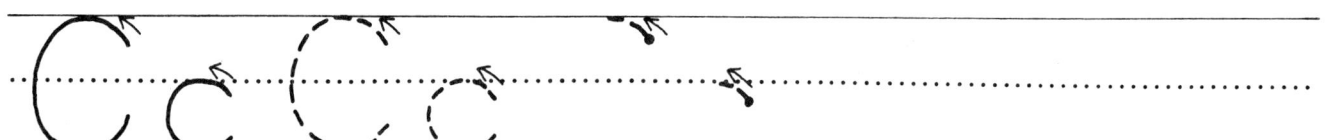

Go over the big **C** and little **c** shapes and finish them.

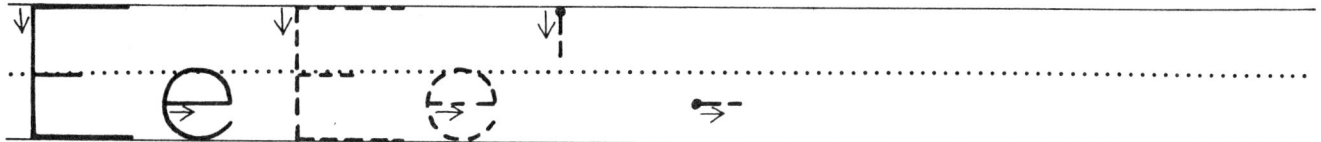

Now go over and finish the big **E**, little **e**, big **T**, little **t**, big **U** and little **u** shapes.

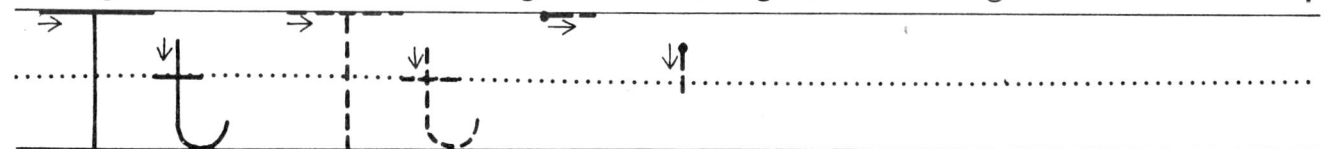

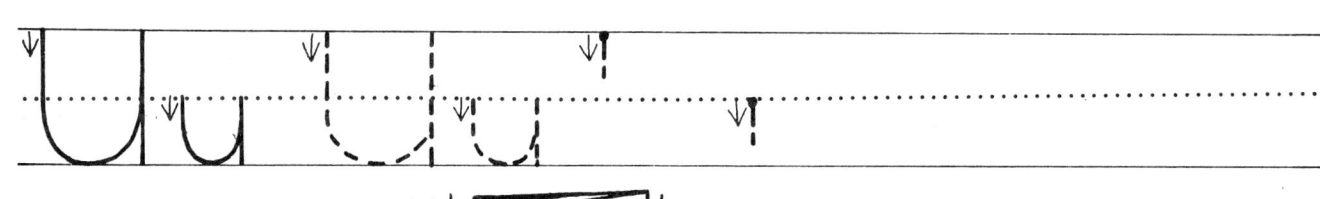

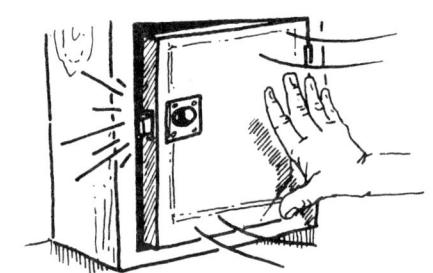

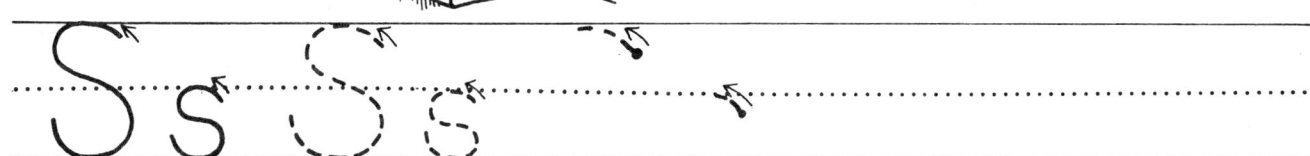

Go over the big **S** and little **s** shapes and finish them.

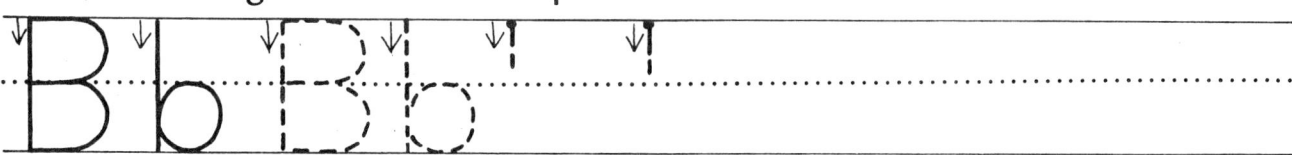

Now go over and finish the big **B**, little **b**, big **P** and little **p** shapes.

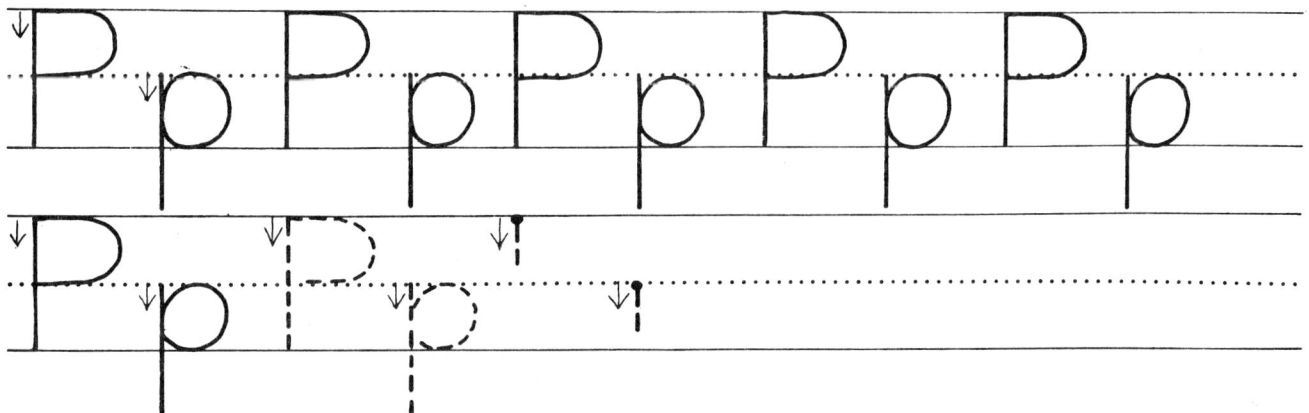

Worksheet 21

Wave pattern revised
Capital letters beside lower case versions — o, a, d, g, q

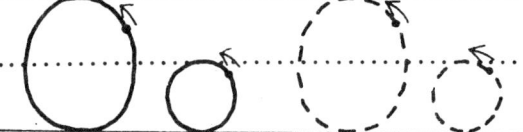

Go over the wave pattern and finish it.

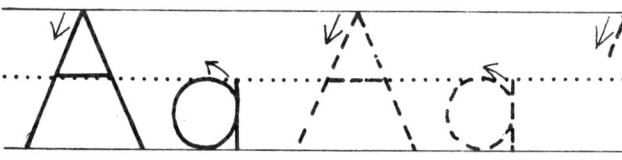

Now go over all the other lines and finish them.

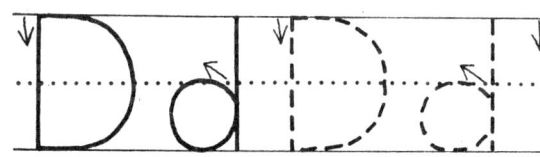

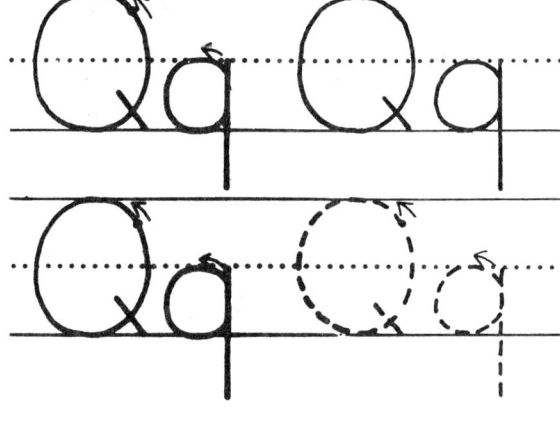

Worksheet 22

a, b, c, d as initial letters of words.

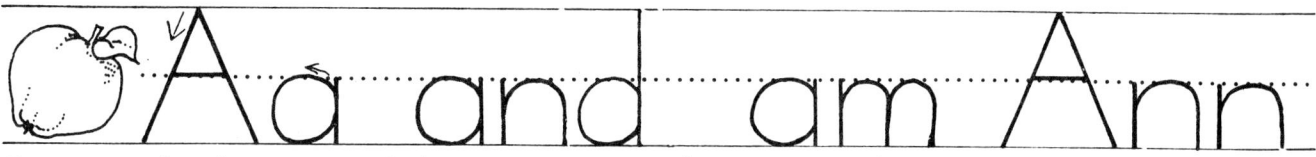

Aa and am Ann

Go over the letters and the words.

Aa

Now copy the letters and the words from the line above.

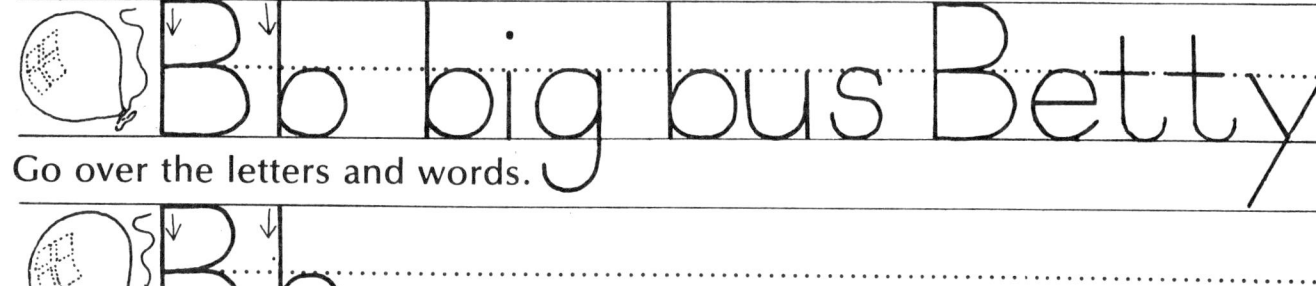

Bb big bus Betty

Go over the letters and words.

Bb

Now copy the letters and words from the line above.

Go over each of the lines below, and then copy them in the space underneath.

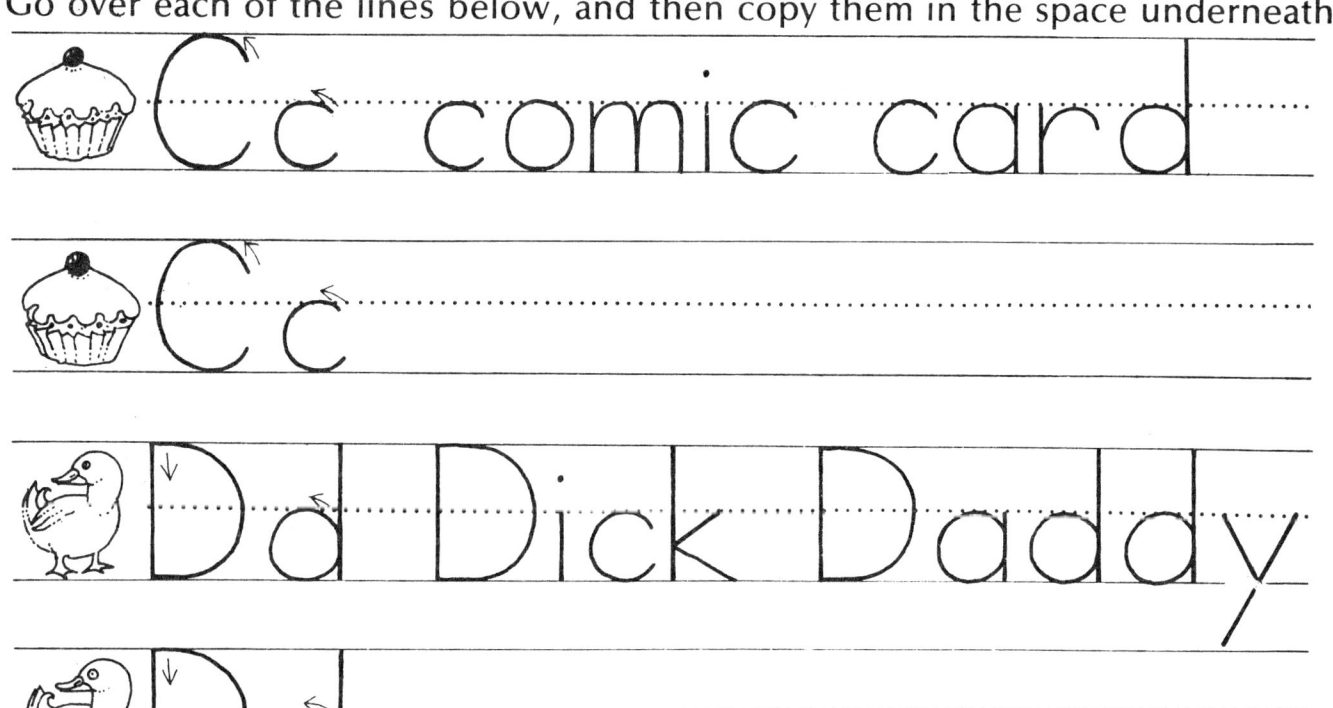

Cc comic card

Cc

Dd Dick Daddy

Dd

Worksheet 23

e, f, g, h as initial letters of words

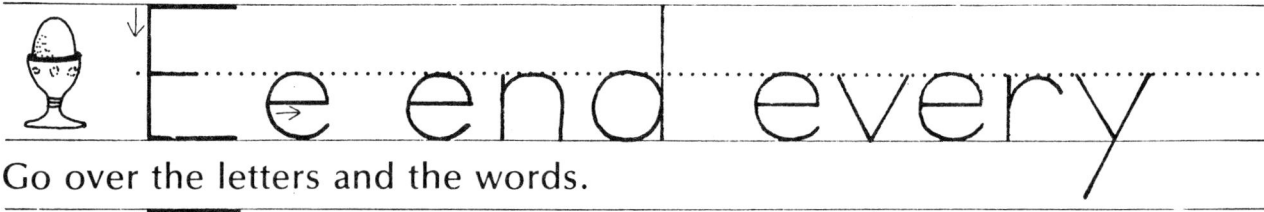

Go over the letters and the words.

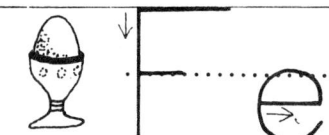

Now copy the letters and words from the line above.

Go over the letters and the words.

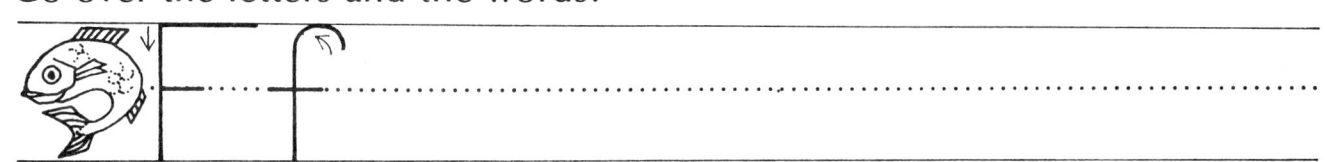

Now copy the letters and words from the line above.

Go over each of the lines below, and then copy them in the spaces underneath.

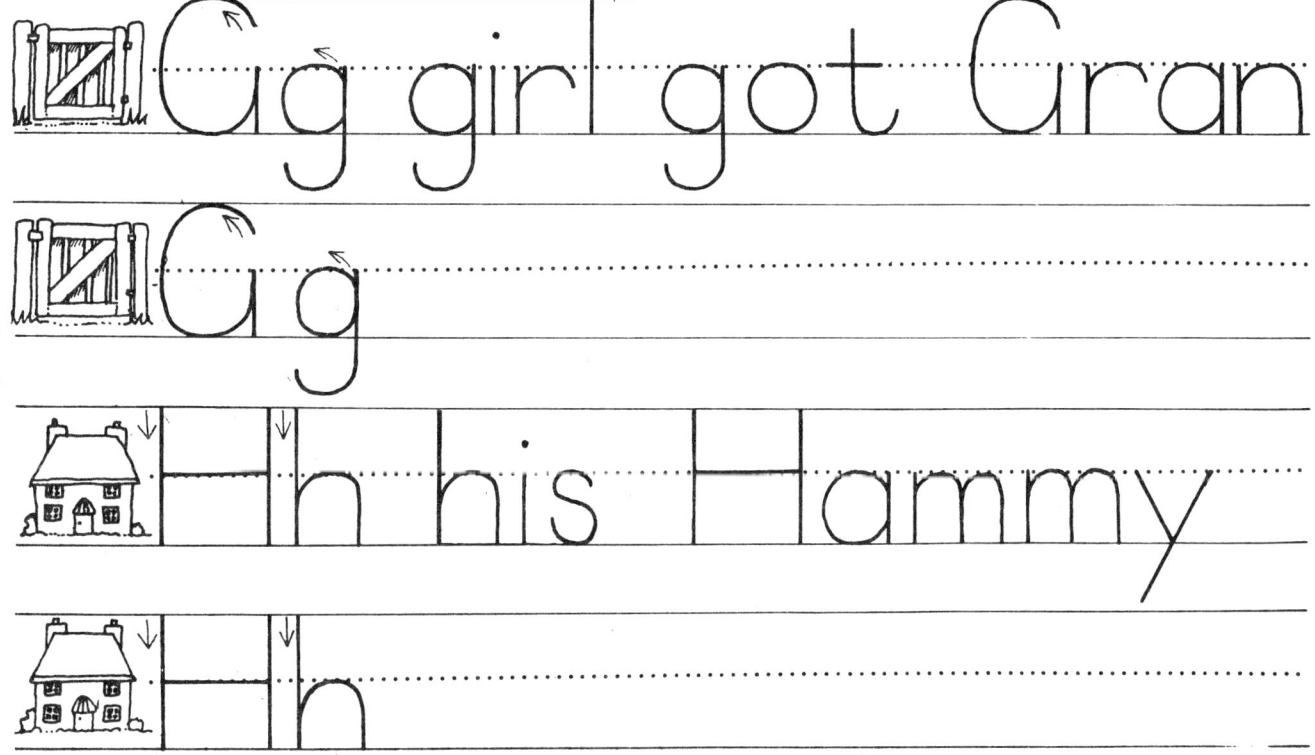

Worksheet 24

i, j, k, l as initial letters of words

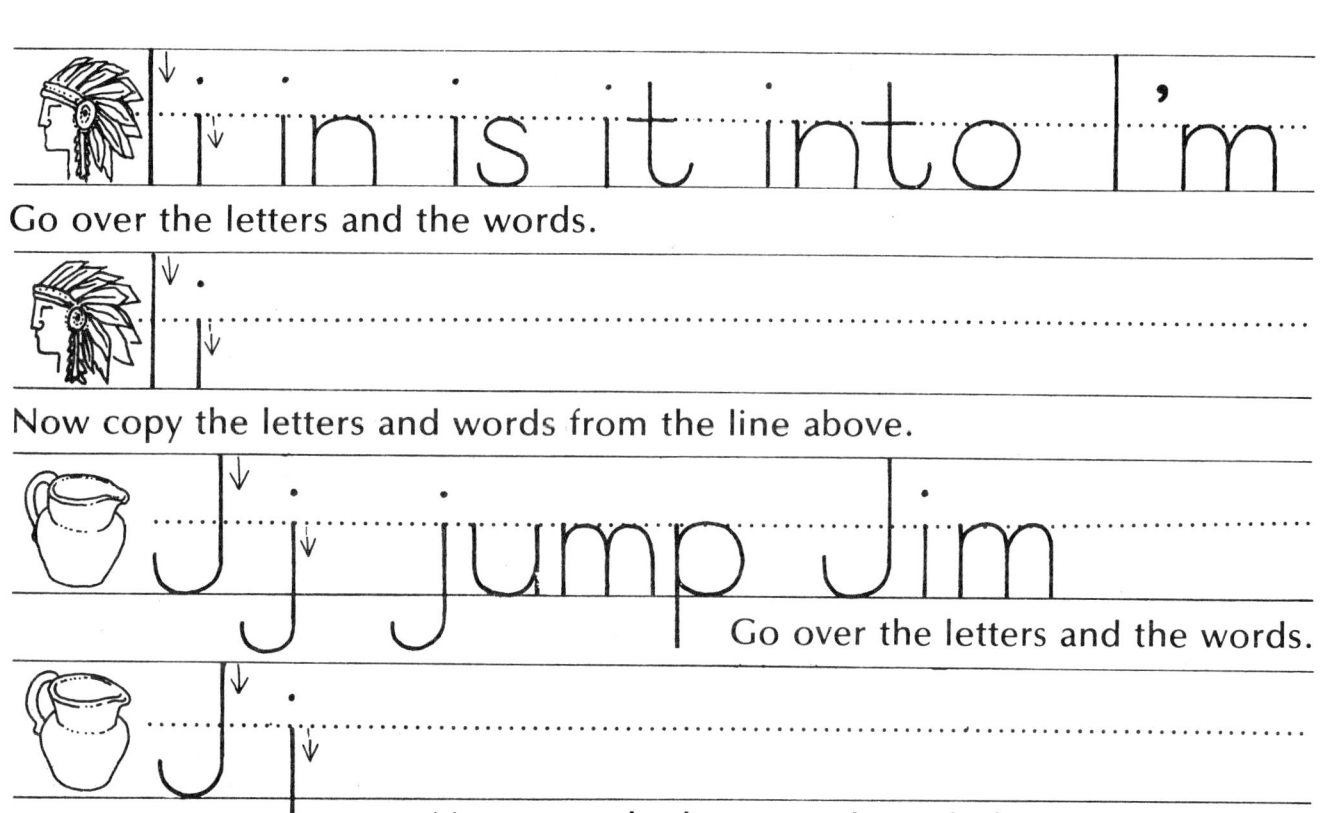

Ii in is it into I'm

Go over the letters and the words.

Ii

Now copy the letters and words from the line above.

Jj jump Jim

Go over the letters and the words.

Jj

Now copy the letters and words from the line above.

Go over each of the lines below, and then copy them in the spaces underneath.

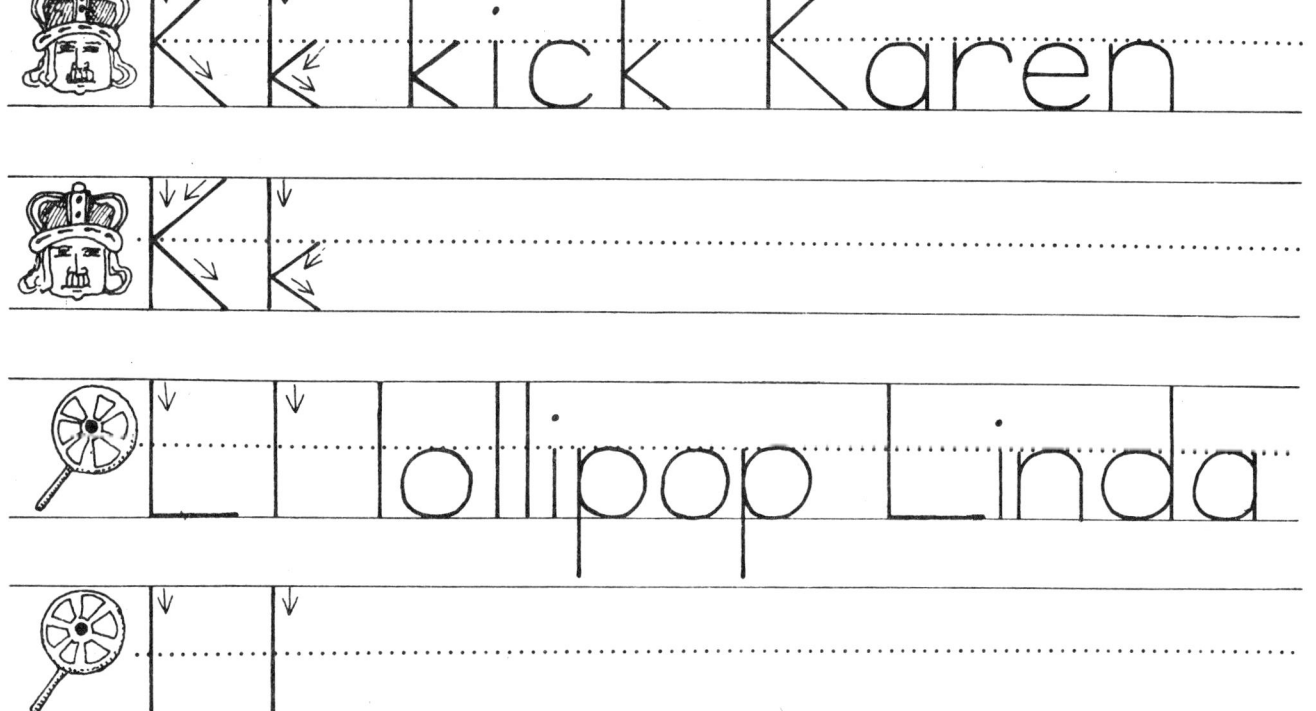

Kk kick Karen

Kk

Ll lollipop Linda

Ll

Worksheet 25

m, n, o, p as initial letters of words

Go over the letters and the words.

Now copy the letters and words from the line above.

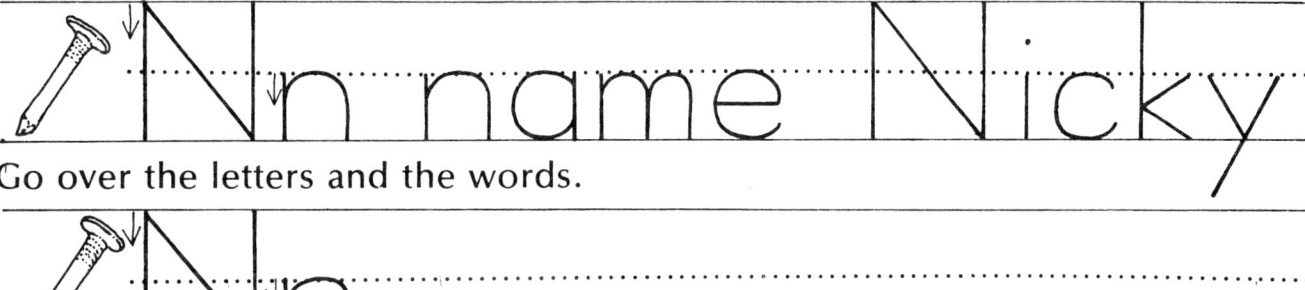

Go over the letters and the words.

Now copy the letters and words from the line above.

Go over each of the lines below, and then copy them in the spaces underneath.

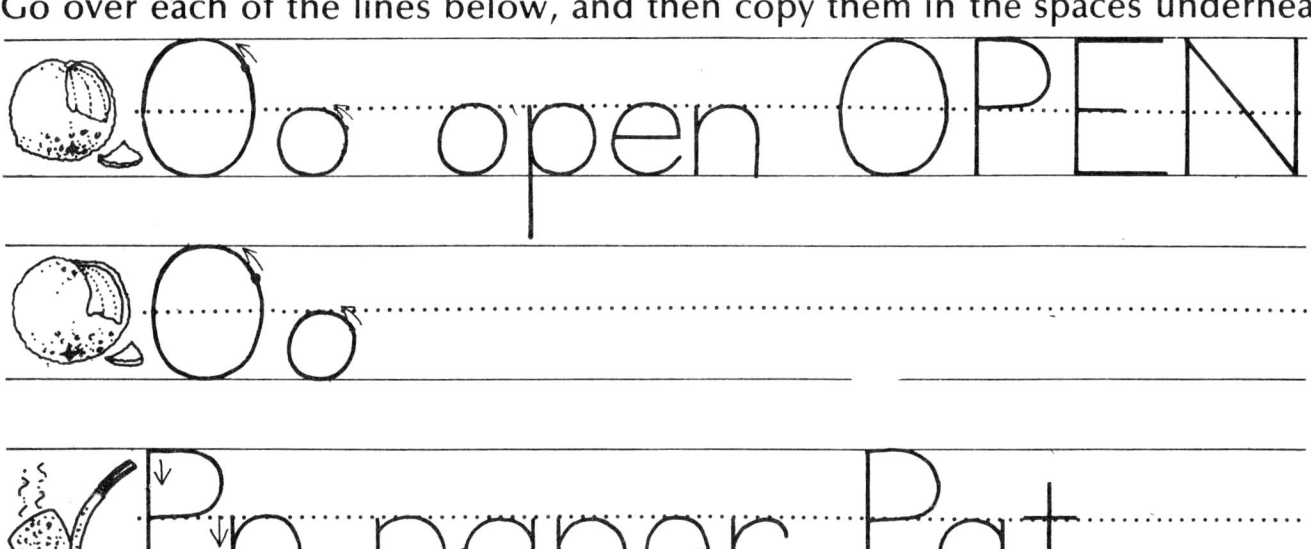

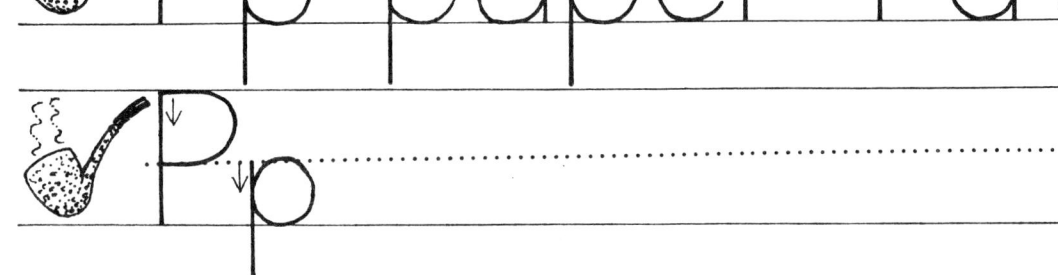

Worksheet 26

q, r, s as initial letters of words

Go over the letters and the words.

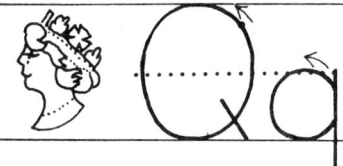

Now copy the letters and words from the line above.

 Rr red Robert

Go over the letters and the words.

Now copy the letters and words from the line above.

Go over each of the lines below, and then copy them in the spaces underneath.

S s song sausages

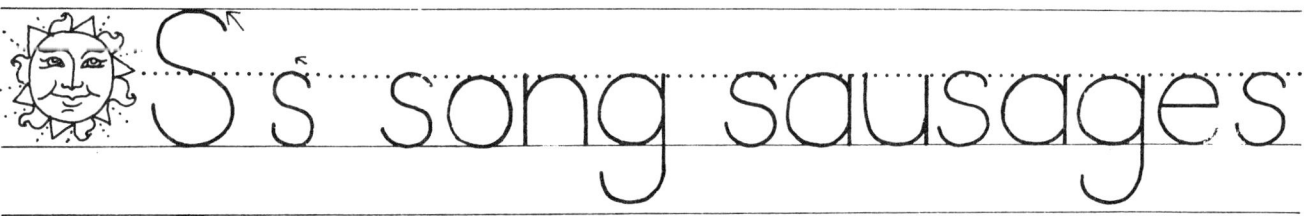

Worksheet 27

t, u, v as initial letters of words

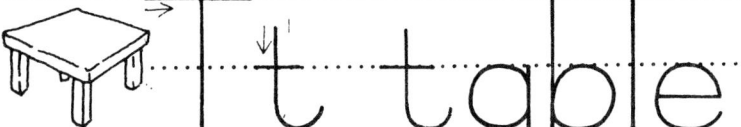 Tt table Tommy

Go over the letters and the words.

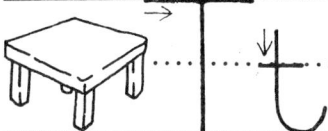 Tt

Now copy the letters and words from the line above.

 Tt teacher to

Go over the letters and the words.

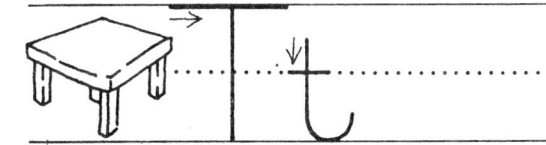 Tt

Now copy the letters and words from the line above.

Go over each of the lines below, and then copy them in the spaces underneath.

 Uu up us Uncle

Vv very Vicky

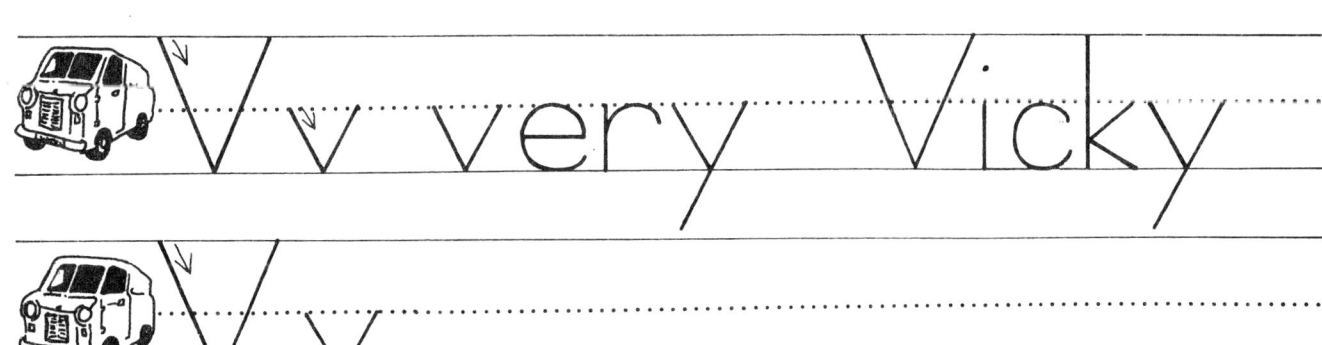

Worksheet 28

w, x, y, z as initial letters of words.

 Ww was we went

Go over the letters and the words.

 Ww

Now copy the letters and words from the line above.

 Xx fox exit EXIT

Go over the letters and the words.

Xx

Now copy the letters and words from the line above.

Go over each of the lines below, and then copy them in the spaces underneath.

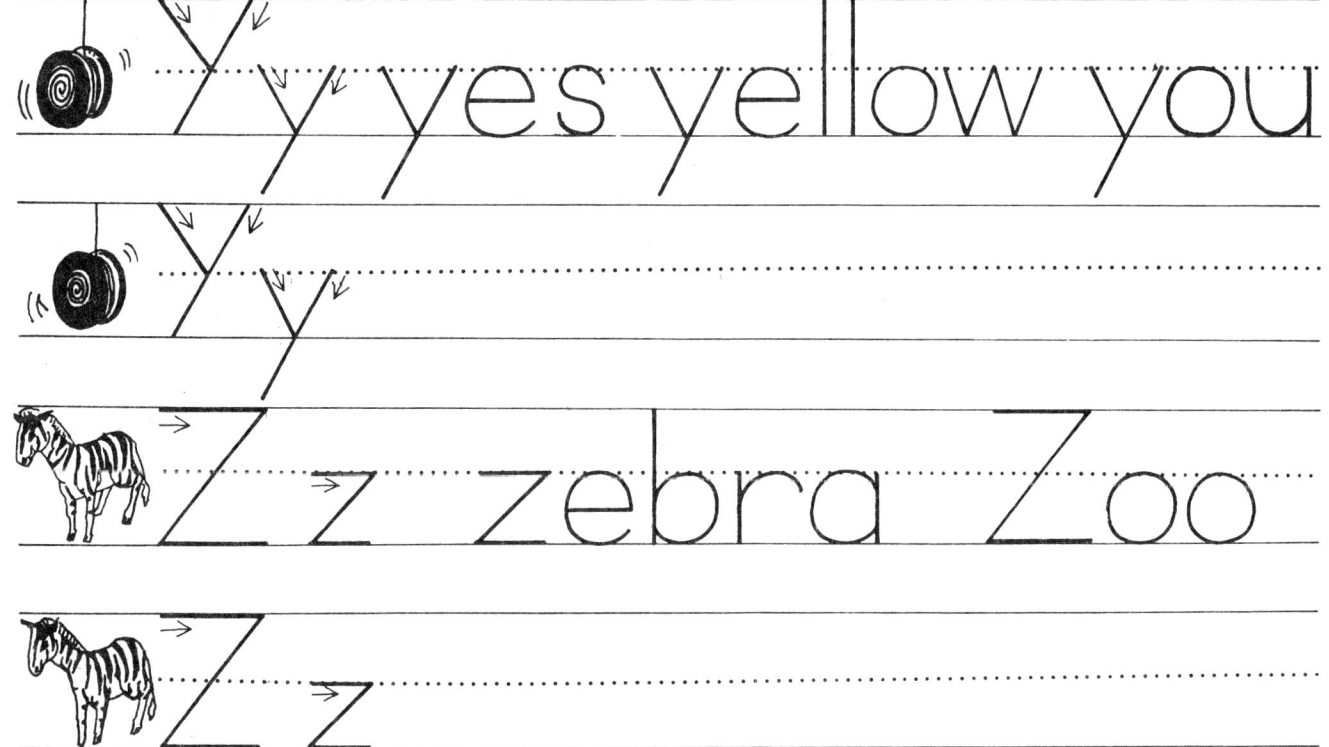 Yy yes yellow you

Yy

Zz zebra Zoo

Zz

Worksheet 29

Letter groups in words — sh, ch, th

sh shop she push

sh

Go over each line, then copy it in the space underneath.

ch chips chocolate

ch

th they then that

th

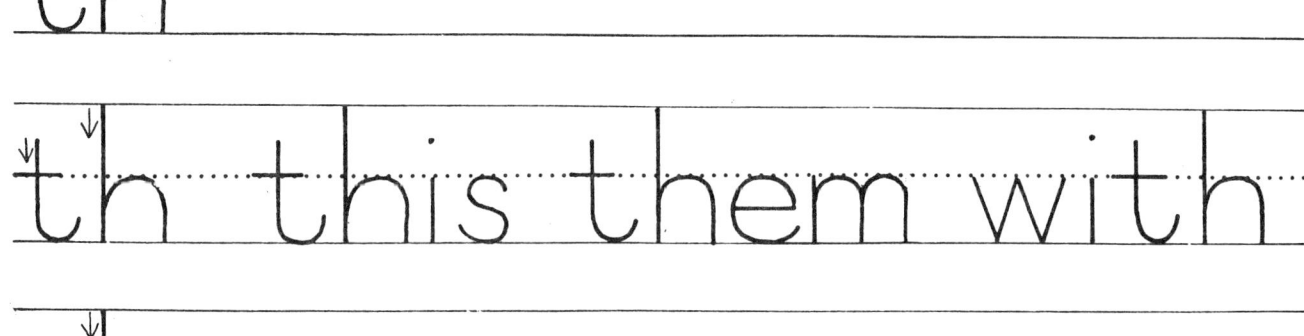

th this them with

th